A Beginner's Guide to Investing in Stocks

Title: A Beginner's Guide to Investing in Stocks: Navigating the 2024 Market

By following the expert advice and guidelines laid out in this comprehensive guide, beginners will be equipped with the necessary knowledge and tools to confidently navigate the stock market in 2024 and beyond. Happy investing!

Introduction to Stock Market Investing

Stock market investing can seem like a daunting and complex world to navigate, but with some basic knowledge and understanding, anyone can begin to build their wealth through investing in stocks. In this article, we will delve into the fundamentals of stock market investing, the benefits it can offer, and common misconceptions that may deter some from taking the leap into the world of investing.

Understanding the Basics of Stocks

At its core, a stock represents a share of ownership in a company. When you purchase a stock, you are essentially buying a small portion of that company, which entitles you to a portion of its profits. Stocks are traded on stock exchanges, such as the New York Stock Exchange or NASDAQ, where buyers and sellers come together to transact shares of publicly traded companies.

Stock prices can fluctuate daily based on a variety of factors, including company performance, economic conditions, and market sentiment. As an investor, it's crucial to conduct thorough research and due diligence before investing in a stock to understand the company's financial health, competitive position, and growth prospects.

Benefits of Investing in Stocks

Investing in stocks can offer several benefits to investors looking to grow their wealth over time. One of the key advantages of investing in stocks is the potential for high returns. Stocks historically have had higher returns compared to other asset classes, such as bonds or cash, over the long term.

Additionally, investing in stocks can help investors hedge against inflation, as stock prices tend to increase over time to keep pace with rising prices. By diversifying your investment portfolio with a mix of stocks, bonds, and other assets, you can help reduce your overall investment risk and potentially earn higher returns.

Common Misconceptions

Despite the benefits of investing in stocks, there are some common misconceptions that may deter individuals from entering the stock market. One of the most prevalent misconceptions is that investing in stocks is like gambling, where investors have no control over their investments and can lose all their money overnight.

In reality, investing in stocks is a long-term commitment that requires research, patience, and discipline. By focusing on investing in quality companies with strong fundamentals and holding onto your investments through market fluctuations, you can build wealth over time and achieve your financial goals.

Another misconception is that stock market investing is only for the wealthy or experienced investors. With the rise of online brokerage platforms and low-cost index funds, investing in stocks has become more accessible to the average individual. By starting small and gradually building your investment portfolio over time, anyone can participate in the stock market and potentially reap the rewards of long-term investing.

In conclusion, stock market investing is a powerful tool for building wealth and achieving financial independence. By understanding the basics of stocks, the benefits of investing in stocks, and dispelling common misconceptions, anyone can begin their journey towards financial success through the stock market.

Notes

Notes

Notes

Notes

Notes

Chapter 2: Setting Financial Goals and Risk Tolerance

Financial planning is a crucial aspect of achieving long-term financial stability. One of the first steps in financial planning is setting clear financial goals. These goals can range from saving for retirement, buying a home, funding your children's education, or simply building wealth for the future. When defining your financial goals, it is important to be specific, measurable, achievable, relevant, and time-bound. This will help you stay focused and motivated on reaching your objectives.

Understanding your risk tolerance is another critical aspect of financial planning. Risk tolerance refers to your ability and willingness to endure fluctuations in the value of your investments. Everyone has a different risk tolerance, which is influenced by factors such as age, financial situation, investment knowledge, and personal comfort level. It is important to assess your risk tolerance before creating an investment strategy to ensure that it aligns with your financial goals and objectives.

Developing an investment strategy involves balancing your financial goals with your risk tolerance. A conservative investor, for example, may prioritize capital preservation over higher returns, while an aggressive investor may be willing to take on more risk in pursuit of greater rewards. Your investment strategy should be tailored to your individual circumstances and objectives, taking into account factors such as time horizon, liquidity needs, tax considerations, and market conditions.

In conclusion, setting financial goals and understanding your risk tolerance are essential components of financial planning. By defining clear objectives and assessing your tolerance for risk, you can develop a personalized investment strategy that aligns with your financial goals and helps you achieve long-term financial success. Remember to regularly review and adjust your financial plan as needed to ensure that it remains on track towards meeting your objectives.

Notes

Notes

Notes

Chapter 3: When it comes to investing, there are several types of investment accounts to consider. Each type of account has its own benefits and considerations, so it's important to understand the differences between them before deciding where to put your money. In this article, we will explore three common types of investment accounts: Individual Brokerage Accounts, Retirement Accounts (such as 401(k) and IRA), and Education Savings Accounts (such as 529 plans).

Individual Brokerage Accounts:
Individual brokerage accounts are the most common type of investment account and are available to anyone who wants to invest in stocks, bonds, mutual funds, and other securities. These accounts are typically opened with a brokerage firm or online brokerage platform and allow investors to buy and sell investments at their discretion.

One of the key benefits of an individual brokerage account is flexibility. Investors have the freedom to choose which investments to buy and when to buy or sell them. Additionally, there are no contribution limits or restrictions on when you can access your funds, making them a popular choice for those who want more control over their investments.

However, individual brokerage accounts do not offer any tax advantages like retirement or education savings accounts. Investors will need to pay taxes on any capital gains or dividends earned in these accounts, which can impact overall returns. It's important to keep this in mind when considering an individual brokerage account as part of your investment strategy.

Retirement Accounts (401(k), IRA):
Retirement accounts are specifically designed to help individuals save for retirement and come with unique tax advantages. Two common types of retirement accounts are 401(k) plans, which are typically offered by employers, and Individual Retirement Accounts (IRAs), which can be opened by individuals independently.

Contributions to 401(k) plans are typically made through automatic payroll deductions, and many employers offer matching contributions up to a certain percentage of your salary. These accounts offer tax-deferred growth, meaning you won't pay taxes on your investments until you begin withdrawing funds in retirement. Additionally, contributions to 401(k) plans are tax-deductible, reducing your taxable income in the year you make the contribution.

IRAs, on the other hand, are independent retirement accounts that offer similar tax benefits as 401(k) plans. Contributions to traditional IRAs are also tax-deductible, and investments grow tax-deferred until withdrawal in retirement. There are different types of IRAs available, including Roth IRAs, which allow for tax-free withdrawals in retirement.

Education Savings Accounts (529):
Education savings accounts, commonly known as 529 plans, are specifically designed to help families save for future education expenses. These accounts offer tax advantages similar to retirement accounts, making them an attractive option for parents saving for their children's college education.

Contributions to 529 plans are made with after-tax dollars, but investments grow tax-free and withdrawals for qualified education expenses are also tax-free. These expenses can include tuition, books, room and board, and other education-related costs. 529 plans may also offer state tax incentives, such as deductions or credits for contributions made to the account.

Overall, the type of investment account you choose will depend on your financial goals, risk tolerance, and time horizon. Individual brokerage accounts offer flexibility but lack tax advantages, while retirement and education savings accounts provide tax benefits but come with restrictions on when funds can be accessed. Consider speaking with a financial advisor to help determine the best investment strategy for your individual needs.

Notes

Notes

Notes

_____

_____

_____

_____

_____

_____

_____

_____

_____

_____

_____

_____

_____

_____

_____

_____

_____

_____

Chapter 4: Choosing Stocks to Invest In

When it comes to investing in the stock market, one of the most important decisions you'll make is choosing which stocks to invest in. There are many different approaches to picking stocks, but three of the most common methods are fundamental analysis, technical analysis, and deciding whether to invest in individual stocks or exchange-traded funds (ETFs).

Fundamental Analysis

Fundamental analysis involves evaluating a company's financial health and potential for growth. This includes examining factors such as revenue, earnings, debt levels, and management performance. By analyzing a company's fundamentals, investors can determine whether a stock is undervalued or overvalued relative to its intrinsic value.

When conducting fundamental analysis, investors should consider a company's competitive position in its industry, growth prospects, and the overall economic environment. By looking at these factors, investors can make informed decisions about which stocks have the potential to outperform the market over the long term.

Technical Analysis

Technical analysis, on the other hand, focuses on analyzing past market data to identify patterns and trends that can help predict future stock price movements. Technical analysts use tools such as charts, graphs, and mathematical indicators to determine when to buy or sell a stock.

Some common technical indicators include moving averages, relative strength index (RSI), and the MACD (moving average convergence divergence). By using these tools, investors can identify trends in a stock's price movements and make decisions based on price patterns and momentum.

Investing in Individual Stocks vs. ETFs

Another important decision for investors is whether to invest in individual stocks or exchange-traded funds (ETFs). Individual stocks offer the potential for high returns, but they also come with higher risk due to the lack of diversification. If a single stock performs poorly, it can have a significant impact on an investor's portfolio.

On the other hand, ETFs offer diversification by holding a basket of stocks or other assets within a single fund. This can help reduce risk and provide more stable returns over time. ETFs are also cost-effective and easy to trade, making them a popular choice for many investors.

Ultimately, the decision to invest in individual stocks or ETFs will depend on your investment goals, risk tolerance, and time horizon. Some investors may prefer the potential for higher returns that individual stocks offer, while others may value the diversification and stability that ETFs provide.

In conclusion, choosing which stocks to invest in requires careful consideration and research. By using fundamental and technical analysis techniques, as well as deciding between individual stocks and ETFs, investors can make informed choices that align with their investment objectives. Remember to always do your own research and consult with a financial advisor before making any investment decisions.

Notes

Notes

Notes

Notes

Chapter 5: Diversification and Asset Allocation

Diversification and asset allocation are two key strategies that can help investors build a strong, well-rounded portfolio. By spreading investments across different asset classes, industries, and geographic regions, investors can reduce the overall risk of their portfolio and increase the potential for long-term growth.

Importance of Diversification

Diversification is often referred to as the "golden rule" of investing because it helps spread risk and minimize the impact of market fluctuations on a portfolio. By investing in a variety of assets, investors can reduce the potential for large losses if one particular asset or investment performs poorly. For example, if a stock market crash negatively impacts equities, investments in bonds or real estate may help balance out losses.

In addition to reducing risk, diversification can also help investors capitalize on different market trends and opportunities. By including a mix of assets in their portfolio, investors can take advantage of potential growth in different sectors or industries, even if others are underperforming.

Building a Balanced Portfolio

Building a balanced portfolio involves allocating investments across different asset classes, such as stocks, bonds, real estate, and commodities, based on individual risk tolerance, financial goals, and time horizon. The goal is to create a mix of assets that can help investors achieve their desired level of return while managing risk effectively.

When building a balanced portfolio, investors should consider factors such as correlation, volatility, and historical performance of different asset classes. For example, if stocks and bonds have a low correlation, adding bonds to a stock-heavy portfolio may help reduce overall risk.

It's important to note that diversification does not guarantee profits or protect against losses, but it can help investors manage risk and potentially improve long-term performance.

Rebalancing Your Portfolio

Once a diversified portfolio is established, it's important for investors to regularly review and rebalance their holdings to maintain the desired asset allocation. Market fluctuations and changes in the performance of different asset classes can cause the portfolio to drift away from its original allocation over time.

Rebalancing involves selling assets that have performed well and buying assets that have underperformed to bring the portfolio back in line with the target allocation. This helps investors stay on track with their financial goals and risk tolerance, while also taking advantage of opportunities to buy assets that may be undervalued.

In conclusion, diversification and asset allocation are essential components of a successful investment strategy. By spreading investments across different asset classes and regularly rebalancing their portfolios, investors can reduce risk, capture potential growth opportunities, and achieve their long-term financial goals.

Notes

Notes

Notes

Notes

Chapter 6: The Role of Market Research and Due Diligence

When it comes to making informed investment decisions, market research and due diligence play a crucial role. By thoroughly analyzing financial statements, company performance, and market trends, investors can gain valuable insights into the potential risks and rewards of a particular investment. In this chapter, we will explore how these key factors can help investors make more informed decisions.

Reading Financial Statements

One of the first steps in conducting due diligence on a potential investment is to carefully examine the company's financial statements. These statements provide a snapshot of the company's financial health, including its revenues, expenses, and profitability. By reviewing the income statement, balance sheet, and cash flow statement, investors can gain a better understanding of the company's financial position and performance.

When analyzing financial statements, investors should pay attention to key financial metrics such as revenue growth, profit margins, and debt levels. These metrics can help investors assess the company's financial stability and growth potential. For example, a company with consistently high revenue growth and healthy profit margins may be a more attractive investment opportunity than a company with stagnant growth and high debt levels.

Analyzing Company Performance

In addition to reviewing financial statements, investors should also analyze the company's performance in relation to its industry peers. By comparing key performance indicators such as revenue growth, market share, and profitability, investors can assess how well the company is performing relative to its competitors. This can help investors identify potential strengths and weaknesses that may impact the company's future growth prospects.

It is also important to consider qualitative factors such as the company's management team, competitive positioning, and growth strategy. A strong management team with a clear vision and track record of success can instill confidence in investors and signal potential for future growth. Additionally, companies that are able to differentiate themselves in a competitive market and adapt to changing market trends may have a competitive advantage over their peers.

Monitoring Market Trends

Lastly, investors should stay informed about market trends and economic conditions that may impact the companies they are considering investing in. By monitoring industry trends, consumer behavior, and macroeconomic factors, investors can anticipate potential risks and opportunities that may affect their investment decisions.

For example, changes in consumer preferences, technological advancements, or regulatory developments can have a significant impact on a company's performance. By staying informed about these trends and understanding how they may impact the company's business model, investors can make more informed investment decisions.

In conclusion, market research and due diligence are essential components of the investment process. By carefully analyzing financial statements, company performance, and market trends, investors can gain valuable insights into the potential risks and rewards of a particular investment. By leveraging these key factors, investors can make more informed decisions that align with their investment objectives and risk tolerance.

Notes

Notes

Notes

Notes

Chapter 7: Managing Your Investments

Setting Stop-Loss Orders

Stop-loss orders are a crucial tool for managing risk in your investments. By setting a pre-determined price at which you will sell your stock, you can protect yourself from significant losses in the event of a market downturn. This allows you to limit your losses and protect your investment portfolio from excessive risk. It's important to carefully consider your stop-loss levels to ensure they align with your risk tolerance and investment goals.

Understanding Stock Volatility

Stock volatility refers to the degree of variation in a stock's trading price. High volatility can lead to rapid price movements, both up and down, presenting the potential for high returns as well as high risks. It's important to understand the level of volatility in the stocks you are investing in, as this can greatly impact your investment decisions. Investors with a lower risk tolerance may want to focus on less volatile stocks to avoid large swings in their portfolio value.

Strategies for Long-Term Growth

Investing for long-term growth requires a different approach than short-term trading. It's important to have a well-thought-out investment plan and stick to your long-term goals in order to maximize returns over time. Diversification is key to managing risk and spreading your investments across different asset classes to minimize potential losses. Dollar-cost averaging involves investing a fixed amount at regular intervals, which can help smooth out the effects of market fluctuations. Additionally, investing in index funds can provide broad market exposure and lower fees, making it a suitable option for long-term investors seeking steady growth.

In conclusion, managing your investments effectively requires a combination of risk management tools, understanding stock volatility, and implementing long-term growth strategies. By setting stop-loss orders, assessing stock volatility, and following a disciplined investment approach, you can navigate the ups and downs of the market and work towards achieving your financial goals. Remember to always conduct thorough research and seek professional advice when making investment decisions to ensure you are on the right track towards building a successful investment portfolio.

Market volatility is a natural part of investing. Prices of stocks, bonds, and other assets can fluctuate on a daily basis, sometimes by significant amounts. When the market is volatile, it can be easy to let your emotions dictate your decisions. However, it is important to stay disciplined and not let fear or greed drive your investment strategy.

In Chapter 8 of most investment guides, you will find valuable information on how to handle market volatility and avoid falling victim to behavioral biases that can lead to poor decision-making. The chapter typically provides tips and strategies for coping with market fluctuations, overcoming emotional decision-making, and staying disciplined in your investment approach.

One of the key principles to remember when dealing with market volatility is to focus on the long-term. It can be tempting to react to every market swing, but this can often lead to buying high and selling low, which is the opposite of what successful investors do. By staying focused on your long-term goals and investment strategy, you can avoid making impulsive decisions that could harm your portfolio.

Another important aspect of handling market volatility is to be aware of your own behavioral biases. These biases, such as loss aversion and overconfidence, can lead investors to make irrational decisions based on emotions rather than facts. By recognizing and understanding these biases, you can take steps to avoid falling into their traps and make more informed investment choices.

Discipline is another key factor in successfully navigating market volatility. It can be easy to get caught up in the excitement of a rising market or the fear of a downturn, but sticking to your investment plan and not deviating from it based on short-term fluctuations is crucial. This is where having a well-defined investment strategy can be particularly helpful, as it provides a roadmap for staying the course even when the market gets rocky.

In conclusion, Chapter 8 of most investment guides provides valuable insights on how to handle market volatility and avoid falling victim to emotional decision-making and behavioral biases. By focusing on the long-term, being aware of your biases, and staying disciplined in your investment strategy, you can weather the ups and downs of the market and increase your chances of long-term investment success.

Notes

Notes

Notes

Notes

Chapter 9 of any comprehensive investment guide is crucial for any investor looking to assess the overall performance of their investments. In this chapter, investors will learn various methods to evaluate the success of their investment decisions, including calculating investment returns, benchmarking their portfolio against market indices, and adjusting their strategy accordingly.

One of the key aspects of evaluating investment performance is calculating investment returns. This involves quantifying the profits or losses made on an investment over a specified period of time. By calculating annualized returns, investors can determine the average rate at which their investments are growing. This information is important for comparing different investment options and tracking the overall success of an investment portfolio.

Benchmarking your portfolio against market indices is another essential component of evaluating investment performance. By comparing the performance of your investments to a relevant market index, such as the S&P 500, investors can gain valuable insights into how well their portfolio is performing relative to the broader market. This information can help investors identify areas where their portfolio may be underperforming and make adjustments to improve overall returns.

Lastly, adjusting your investment strategy based on the evaluation of investment performance is critical for long-term success in the market. By analyzing the data from calculating investment returns and benchmarking your portfolio, investors can identify weaknesses in their current strategy and make necessary changes to optimize returns. This may involve rebalancing asset allocations, diversifying investments, or making strategic changes to individual holdings.

In conclusion, Chapter 9: Evaluating Investment Performance provides investors with the tools and strategies needed to assess the success of their investment decisions. By calculating investment returns, benchmarking their portfolio, and adjusting their investment strategy accordingly, investors can make informed decisions to optimize their investment performance and achieve their financial goals.

As individuals seek to continue their learning and growth in the realm of investing, there are a plethora of resources available to guide them on their journey. Chapter 10 of many investment books and courses often delve into these resources, providing readers with the tools they need to further their knowledge and expertise in the field. In this article, we will explore three key resources for continued learning and growth in investing: online investment platforms, professional investment advice, and books, blogs, and podcasts.

Online investment platforms have revolutionized the way individuals can invest their money. With just a few clicks, investors can access a wealth of information, research, and analysis to make informed decisions about where to put their money. These platforms provide users with real-time data on market trends, investment options, and portfolio performance, allowing them to stay up-to-date on the latest developments in the financial world. Additionally, online investment platforms often offer tools and resources, such as calculators and investment guides, to help investors make smart investment choices. Whether you are a seasoned investor or new to the world of investing, online investment platforms can be a valuable resource for continued learning and growth.

Professional investment advice is another valuable resource for investors looking to expand their knowledge and skills. Financial advisors and wealth managers have the expertise and experience to help individuals navigate the complexities of the investment world and develop a personalized investment strategy that aligns with their financial goals. These professionals can provide guidance on asset allocation, risk management, and investment selection, helping investors make sound decisions that will lead to long-term financial success. Seeking out professional investment advice can provide individuals with the confidence and peace of mind they need to make informed investment decisions and achieve their financial objectives.

In addition to online investment platforms and professional investment advice, books, blogs, and podcasts can also be excellent resources for continued learning and growth in investing. There are countless books written by renowned investors and financial experts that provide valuable insights and strategies for successful investing. Blogs and podcasts offer a more informal and accessible way to consume information, with experts sharing their knowledge and experiences in an engaging and relatable format. By immersing oneself in the world of investing through these resources, individuals can expand their knowledge, stay informed on market trends, and learn from the successes and failures of others.

In conclusion, Chapter 10 of many investment books and courses often emphasizes the importance of seeking out resources for continued learning and growth in investing. Online investment platforms, professional investment advice, and books, blogs, and podcasts are just a few of the resources available to individuals looking to further their knowledge and expertise in the field. By taking advantage of these resources, investors can stay informed, make smart investment decisions, and ultimately achieve their financial goals. Whether you are a novice investor or a seasoned pro, there is always more to learn and discover in the world of investing.

Notes

Notes

Notes

Notes

The document provides a comprehensive guide to Stock Market Investing with a focus on various key topics. Chapter 1 introduces readers to the basics of stocks, highlighting the benefits and common misconceptions of investing in stocks. Chapter 2 emphasizes the importance of setting financial goals, understanding risk tolerance, and developing an investment strategy. Chapter 3 explores different types of investment accounts such as individual brokerage accounts, retirement accounts, and education savings accounts.

In Chapter 4, readers learn about choosing stocks to invest in through fundamental and technical analysis, as well as the differences between investing in individual stocks versus ETFs. Chapter 5 discusses the significance of diversification and asset allocation in building a balanced portfolio. Chapter 6 covers the role of market research and due diligence in making informed investment decisions.

Chapter 7 focuses on managing investments through setting stop-loss orders, understanding stock volatility, and implementing strategies for long-term growth. Chapter 8 addresses handling market volatility and behavioral biases, emphasizing the importance of staying disciplined in one's investment strategy. Chapter 9 delves into evaluating investment performance, with guidance on calculating returns, benchmarking portfolios, and making adjustments to strategies.

The document concludes with Chapter 10 which provides resources for continued learning and growth in stock market investing, including online investment platforms, professional advice, and recommendations for books, blogs, and podcasts. Overall, the document serves as a comprehensive guide for individuals looking to build and manage a successful investment portfolio in the stock market.

Notes

Notes

Notes

Notes

Notes

Notes

Notes

Notes

Notes

Notes

Notes

Notes

Notes

Notes

Notes

Notes

Notes

Notes

Notes

Notes

Notes

Notes

Notes

Notes

Notes

www.ingramcontent.com/pod-product-compliance
Lightning Source LLC
Chambersburg PA
CBHW081000290526
45795CB00009B/3012